SEA LIFE GUIDEBOOK

Courtney Acampora

Silver Dolphin

Silver Dolphin Books
An imprint of Printers Row Publishing Group
A division of Readerlink Distribution Services, LLC
10350 Barnes Canyon Road, Suite 100, San Diego, CA 92121
www.silverdolphinbooks.com

Manufactured, printed, and assembled in Heshan, China.
First printing, July 2019. HH/07/19.
23 22 21 20 19 1 2 3 4 5

Written by Courtney Acampora
Designed by Dynamo, Ltd.

TABLE OF CONTENTS

DIVE INTO THE OCEAN

Oceans are very important to life on Earth. They hold 97 percent of Earth's water and cover most of Earth's surface. The richest variety of life on Earth is found within the oceans.

THE IMPORTANCE OF OCEANS

We would not be able to live if it were not for oceans. They are part of the water cycle, which moves water from the ocean to the sky, and comes back to Earth in the form of rain or snow. The water that is on Earth is the only water we will ever have, so it is important to keep our oceans clean.

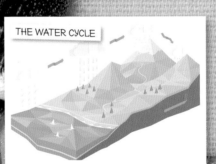

THE WATER CYCLE

EARTH'S FIVE OCEANS

The water that covers most of Earth is divided into five oceans: the Pacific, Atlantic, Indian, Arctic, and Southern (Antarctic). Whether the ocean is cold and icy or warm and tropical, many different kinds of animals call the ocean home.

ARCTIC OCEAN

PACIFIC OCEAN

ATLANTIC OCEAN

PACIFIC OCEAN

INDIAN OCEAN

SOUTHERN OCEAN

WHY ARE OCEANS SALTY?

Volcanoes have played a large part in the formation of Earth's surface. The lava, rock, and ash from a volcanic eruption dissolve into salt and other minerals that become new soil. When it rains, the water picks up salt from the soil. This salty water eventually finds its way into streams and rivers that empty into the ocean.

RIVER DELTA

HABITAT HOMES

Earth's oceans have many different types of **habitats**. A habitat is a home for plants and animals. The shallow waters of tide pools provide the perfect habitat for sea stars and shorebirds. Tangled kelp forests are home to fish and sea otters. The icy cold habitat of the Arctic is home to polar bears and narwhals.

SEA LIFE

The five oceans are home to a rich variety of sea life. From the giant blue whale to the intelligent dolphin to the ferocious great white shark, sea creatures in all shapes, sizes, and colors live in every part of the ocean. Get ready to dive in and explore sea life!

SEA STARS

SEA OTTER

GREAT WHITE SHARK

OCEAN HABITATS

The ocean is one continuous string of habitats. Each habitat flows into the next. Some animals spend their entire lives in one habitat, such as a humpback whale in the open ocean or a clown fish in a tropical reef. Other animals move between habitats, such as the sea lion that may swim in the open ocean, feed at the seashore, and rest on the rocky shore.

TIDE POOL

DEEP SEA

OPEN OCEAN

ICY WATER

ROCKY SHORE

COASTAL WATERS

SEASHORE

CORAL REEF

KELP FOREST

TIDE POOL

Tide pools are formed in rocks along the shore that fill with water as the tide comes in. Sea stars, anemones, sea urchins, and crabs are just a few of the many creatures that are found in these shallow pools.

TIDE POOL

SEABIRDS AT LOW TIDE

COLORFUL TIDE POOLS

Colorful sea stars can be seen attached to the sides of tide pools. Hermit crabs like to scuttle around the shallow waters. Snails use their muscular foot to move across the tide pools. Seabirds love tide pools too—they feast on animals exposed during low tide.

TIDE IN, TIDE OUT

Because of the moon's enormous size, it pulls the oceans' water toward and away from it. When the moon's gravity pulls the water toward shore, it is high tide. When it draws it away from shore, it is low tide.

RISE AND FALL

Twice a day, the **sea level** rises and falls along the seashore. The change in sea level is called the tide and is caused by the moon's gravity.

When the tide goes out, the holes in the rocks along the shore are filled with water, which form tide pools.

ANIMAL PROFILES

SEA STAR

SIZE: UP TO 16 INCHES ACROSS AND WEIGHING UP TO 11 POUNDS

FAVORITE FOOD: CLAMS AND OYSTERS

Sea stars can be bright colors such as orange, blue, or purple. They can be as small as a human hand or can grow to be three feet long. They have **tube feet** that help them crawl and stick to surfaces.

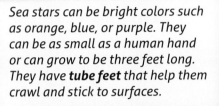

SEA STARS

If one of a sea star's arms is broken off by a **predator**, the sea star can grow a new arm in its place. Some sea stars' arms even grow into a whole new sea star!

SEA ANEMONE

SIZE: UP TO 6 FEET ACROSS

FAVORITE FOOD: SMALL FISH, SHRIMP, MUSSELS, PLANKTON

SEA URCHIN

SIZE: UP TO 4 INCHES ACROSS

FAVORITE FOOD: ALGAE

SEA URCHIN

Sea urchins are often called "hedgehogs of the sea" because of the many spines that cover their body. Like a sea star's tube feet, the spines help the sea urchin move around the tide pool.

Sea anemones come in all different shapes, sizes, and colors. They can be found in tide pools and coral reefs in bright colors such as green, purple, and orange.

CRAB

SIZE: UP TO 1 FOOT ACROSS

FAVORITE FOOD: ALGAE, WORMS, MOLLUSKS, OTHER CRUSTACEANS

CRAB IN TIDE POOL

Crabs are **crustaceans** that can be seen scuttling around tide pools or along the shore during low tide. Instead of having bones on the inside of their body, they have a hard outer shell for protection.

SEASHORE

The seashore is the environment where the ocean meets land. It is made of shallow waters that are the home to creatures that have adapted to the constant rise and fall of the tide. With the rising of the tide, the nooks and crannies of the tide pools fill with water. Crabs scuttle along the shore. Birds walk along the wet sand searching for food, or float atop the water. Seaweed washes ashore and becomes a hiding spot for small creatures. The seashore is a unique environment that is home to life on both land and sea.

SOARING SEABIRDS

While many sea creatures spend their time in the shallow waters of the shore, birds also find their home by the sea— flying above it, floating on it, and standing and diving in it.

Albatrosses can be found all over the world near oceans. They can live to be 50 years old, and have the longest wingspan of any bird: up to 11 feet! Albatrosses fly above the ocean for hours or sometimes float on the ocean surface for a rest from flying.

ALBATROSS

SIZE: WINGSPAN UP TO 11 FEET AND WEIGHING UP TO 22 POUNDS

FAVORITE FOOD: SQUID, FISH

HABITAT: SOUTH ATLANTIC, PACIFIC, AND SOUTHERN OCEANS

ANIMAL PROFILES: SEABIRDS

Flamingos are pink birds with long legs and necks that live in warm, shallow lakes and lagoons along the seashore. Sometimes, thousands of flamingos live together.

PELICAN

SIZE: 6 FEET AND WEIGHING UP TO 30 POUNDS

FAVORITE FOOD: FISH

HABITAT: COASTLINES, RIVERS, AND LAKES AROUND THE WORLD

Pelicans are known for the pouch located under their bill that they use to catch fish. Pelicans dive into the water, scoop up the fish, drain out the water, and then swallow the fish whole.

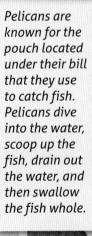

FLAMINGO

SIZE: UP TO 4.5 FEET TALL AND WEIGHING UP TO 9 POUNDS

FAVORITE FOOD: SHRIMP

HABITAT: SOUTHERN WARM COASTAL WATERS OF AFRICA, SOUTHWEST ASIA, AND THE CARIBBEAN

COASTAL WATERS

When it rains, the water is either absorbed into the soil or it drains into a stream or river. Eventually, those freshwater streams and rivers will make their way into a pond or lake, or most often, to the ocean. Coastal waters are the places where the streams and rivers feed into the ocean.

WETLANDS

Wetlands are shallow bodies of water located near a river, lake, or stream and can be made up of both freshwater and salt water. Because of its rich soil, many different types of water plants grow in wetlands.

DELTAS

Wetlands are found by deltas. Deltas are formed when rivers empty their water into oceans, lakes, or another river. Deltas can be different shapes based on the amount of dirt and sand left behind by the river. Rich minerals in the flowing rivers collect in deltas. These rich minerals cause many plants to flourish; these plants feed the animals that live there.

NILE RIVER DELTA

DRAINING DELTAS

Deltas are located all over the world. Some of the world's famous rivers, such as the Amazon, Mississippi, and Nile, have large deltas that connect to oceans.

Freshwater and salt water can both be important to the lives of some fish. Salmon spend part of their lives in freshwater and the rest in salt water. Deltas are the important connection between oceans and rivers, and salmon use them to migrate to and from these bodies of water.

ANIMAL PROFILES: SALMON

RETURNING HOME

Salmon lay eggs in freshwater rivers and streams. When the baby salmon hatch, they swim downstream and into the ocean, where they spend most of their lives. Later, the salmon return to the freshwater stream where they were born to mate and lay their own eggs.

PACIFIC SALMON

SIZE: UP TO 5 FEET LONG AND WEIGHING UP TO 110 POUNDS

FAVORITE FOOD: INSECTS, PLANKTON, FISH, SHRIMP

HABITAT: NORTHERN PACIFIC OCEAN

The annual salmon run is the time when salmon leave the ocean and migrate upstream to freshwater streams. This popular **migration** also attracts grizzly bears. Groups of grizzly bears wade in the streams to catch and eat the migrating salmon.

Manatees and dugongs are large, gentle **mammals** that live in warm coastal waters and rivers. Like other mammals, manatees and dugongs have to come to the surface to breathe. They spend their lives in the water but have to come up for air every three or four minutes.

MANATEE

DUGONG

MANATEES, DUGONGS, AND ELEPHANTS?

Manatees and dugongs may look like whales, but they are more closely related to elephants. Like elephants, manatees and dugongs are large and weigh over 1,000 pounds. They eat about one-tenth of their body weight a day, which is about 100 pounds of plants!

According to legend, manatees and dugongs were thought to be mermaids by sailors. Those must have been some big mermaids!

ENDANGERED ANIMALS

Endangered means at risk of extinction. Manatees and dugongs are endangered animals. Major threats to manatees are watercraft and boat propellers, which can injure manatees. Dugongs are threatened by habitat loss. If their habitat is decreased, they will not have enough food to live.

MANATEES FEEDING

MANATEE

LENGTH: UP TO 13 FEET

WEIGHT: UP TO 3,650 POUNDS

HABITAT: WARM COASTAL WATERS AND RIVERS ALONG THE COAST OF NORTH AND SOUTH AMERICA AND AFRICA

FAVORITE FOOD: FLOATING PLANTS, MANGROVE LEAVES, SEA GRASSES

SEA COWS

Manatees are sometimes called "sea cows" because they spend their day eating grass just like cows on land, except manatees eat sea grass.

MANGROVES

DUGONG

LENGTH: UP TO 10 FEET

WEIGHT: UP TO 1,100 POUNDS

HABITAT: WARM COASTAL WATERS OF EAST AFRICA AND AUSTRALIA

FAVORITE FOOD: SEA GRASSES

DUGONG DIFFERENCES

Unlike manatees, dugongs have a tail like that of a whale. Dugongs only live in the ocean, while manatees can be found in coastal waters and rivers.

MANATEES AND MANGROVES

Mangrove refers to many types of trees that are able to grow in salt water. They grow in coastal channels and winding rivers. Mangroves are forests on the water, creating shelter for the animals swimming beneath them. The leaves of the mangrove tree are a favorite food of manatees.

CORAL REEFS

Corals are brightly colored, soft-bodied **polyps**, similar to a sea anemone. One end is hard and solid, and the other end has a mouth surrounded by a ring of stinging **tentacles**.

They come in all different shapes, colors, and sizes. Some corals are hard and rigid, and others are soft and flexible.

CORAL COLONIES

Corals are not often found alone—they live in groups, or colonies. One end of a coral attaches itself to a hard underwater surface. When they attach to a hard surface, the corals will multiply and connect to each other, creating a **colony**.

BRAIN CORAL

PILLAR CORAL

STAGHORN CORAL

Corals are the oldest living organisms found in the oceans. Most of the coral reefs we see today are between 5,000 to 10,000 years old. The first coral reefs were formed over 240 million years ago!

THE MAKING OF A CORAL REEF

When a coral colony forms, the corals' skeletons connect together, making a reef. Coral reefs form slowly, growing only a few inches in one year.

THE IMPORTANCE OF CORAL REEFS

Coral reefs cover less than 1 percent of Earth's surface. But they are home to 25 percent of all the ocean species on the planet!

EARTH'S CORAL REEFS

THE WORLD'S LARGEST CORAL REEF

The Great Barrier Reef off the northeastern coast of Australia has been growing for more than 20,000 years. In that time, it has grown to be 1,600 miles long. It is so big that it can be seen from outer space!

GREAT BARRIER REEF

AUSTRALIA

HIDE-AND-SEEK

When coral reefs formed thousands of years ago, they left small caves and openings that became the perfect homes and hiding spots for sea creatures. From sea stars to eels to sea anemones, coral reefs are home to a rich variety of sea life.

CORAL REEFS
ANIMAL PROFILES

Puffer fish have the ability to change their body form when they are threatened. If a predator is near, a puffer fish will swallow water to inflate like a ball. When it puffs up, dangerous spines stand out from its body. If it is swallowed, it can poison the predator.

PUFFER FISH

SIZE: UP TO 3 FEET LONG

FAVORITE FOOD: ALGAE, SHELLFISH, INVERTEBRATES

HABITAT: WARM OCEAN WATERS AROUND THE WORLD

Clown fish are bright orange fish with white stripes that are found swimming among coral reefs.

CLOWN FISH HOMES

CLOWN FISH

SIZE: UP TO 6 INCHES LONG

FAVORITE FOOD: ALGAE

HABITAT: SHALLOW WATERS OF THE WESTERN PACIFIC OCEAN

Sea anemones are colorful creatures related to coral and jellyfish. They attach to rocks and wait for their **prey** to swim close. Once the prey is close enough, the sea anemone stings its prey with its poisonous tentacles. Clown fish are covered in mucus that protects them from anemones' poisonous tentacles. Because other fish would be stung, anemones keep clown fish safe from predators. Clown fish and sea anemones have a great relationship—the clown fish is protected from predators by the sea anemone and the sea anemone gets to snack on the clown fish's scraps.

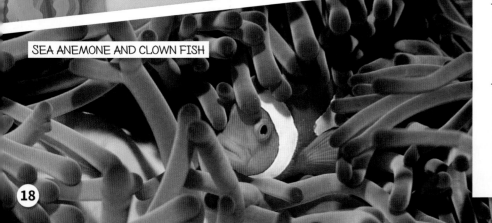

SEA ANEMONE AND CLOWN FISH

PARROT FISH

SIZE: UP TO 4 FEET LONG

FAVORITE FOOD: ALGAE

HABITAT: WARM WATERS OF THE CARIBBEAN AND WEST ATLANTIC OCEAN

Parrot fish are brightly colored and their mouth looks like a parrot's beak. To protect themselves when they sleep, parrot fish cover themselves in a cocoon made of mucus. It helps mask their scent from predators.

QUEEN ANGELFISH

SIZE: UP TO 18 INCHES LONG

FAVORITE FOOD: SPONGES AND ALGAE

HABITAT: WARM WATERS OF THE CARIBBEAN AND WEST ATLANTIC OCEANS

Queen angelfish are bright blue fish found around coral reefs. They are named for the black spot on their head that resembles a crown. They have bright yellow fins, with orange and purple on their bodies. Although they are quite colorful, queen angelfish blend in with the vibrant coral reefs.

The lionfish's showy striped fins may look beautiful, but these needlelike fins actually deliver a powerful sting. Its venomous fins are only used in defense. To catch its prey, a lionfish will **camouflage** itself against the colorful coral reef and strike out with lightning-fast speed to catch a small fish or shrimp.

LIONFISH

SIZE: UP TO 15 INCHES LONG

FAVORITE FOOD: SMALL FISH AND SHRIMP

HABITAT: CORAL REEFS OF THE SOUTHWESTERN PACIFIC OCEAN

CORAL REEFS
ANIMAL PROFILES

SEA HORSE

SIZE: UP TO 14 INCHES TALL

HABITAT: SHALLOW WARM WATERS AROUND THE WORLD

FAVORITE FOOD: PLANKTON, BRINE SHRIMP

Sea horses are unique animals that were named because their faces look a bit like horses' heads. These fish have tiny fins, which make them slow swimmers. To keep them from drifting away, they curl their tails around sea grasses. Sea horses' coloring helps them to blend in with the same grasses they wrap themselves around. This camouflage makes it harder for predators to spot them.

SEA HORSE FATHERS

Sea horses are one of the few animal species in which the father carries the babies instead of the mother. The mother places her eggs in a pouch located on the front of the father's body. The father swims around with a bulging belly until the baby sea horses are born.

The leafy sea dragon is related to the sea horse. Like sea horses, the male leafy sea dragon carries the eggs in a pouch located under its tail.

LEAFY SEA DRAGON

SIZE: UP TO 14 INCHES LONG

HABITAT: WARM WATERS OF THE SOUTHERN COAST OF AUSTRALIA

FAVORITE FOOD: SMALL CRUSTACEANS

This brown-and-yellow fish has a body that makes it look like seaweed or kelp. Leafy sea dragons also sway gently with the plants in the current, making it even harder to tell them apart.

YELLOW-BELLIED SEA SNAKE

SIZE: UP TO 5 FEET LONG

HABITAT: WARM WATERS OF THE INDIAN AND PACIFIC OCEANS

FAVORITE FOOD: FISH AND FISH EGGS

Sea snakes are snakes with a flattened tail that helps propel them through the water. They live in shallow and coastal waters. Their fangs can deliver highly poisonous bites.

MORAY EEL

SIZE: UP TO 13 FEET LONG

HABITAT: WARM COASTAL WATERS AROUND THE WORLD

FAVORITE FOOD: FISH, OCTOPUSES, CRUSTACEANS

Moray eels look like snakes, but they are fish. When they swim, they move their bodies back and forth similar to how snakes slither on land. Giant moray eels can grow up to 13 feet long and move through the water by flexing their entire body. They can swim both forward and backward.

Giant moray eels love to hide in the holes of coral reefs. When their favorite foods swim by, they dart out and grab the prey with their large mouth and razor-sharp teeth.

ROCKY SHORE

The rocky shore is a habitat for animals that live in, under, and around rocks on the coast. Because of the tides, the animals live in an environment where the sea level is constantly changing. The animals that live at the rocky shore have adapted to the rising and falling water level.

Some animals, such as seals, spend time on the rocky shore when they aren't in the water. Octopuses hide in spaces between underwater rocks. Barnacles and mussels attach to the rocks so they aren't pulled out with the tides.

ROCKY WATERS

The animals that live along the rocky shore are sometimes exposed to the sun and have little water when the tide is low. At other times, they are pounded with waves.

RICH ROCKY SHORE

Plants along the rocky shore are an important part of the **food chain**. A food chain is a series of living things in which the next lower member is used as a source of food. Important nutrients and energy are passed to each animal or plant in a food chain.

The plants of the rocky shore get their energy from sunlight. The fish and other plant-eaters get energy from eating the plants. Then the birds and animals that eat the fish get their energy and nutrients.

While many creatures can be found submerged in water along the rocky shore, birds often fly above and along it. Rocky shores are important nesting and feeding grounds for birds.

ANIMAL PROFILES: MOLLUSKS

Mollusks are soft-bodied creatures that live along the rocky shore. These animals, such as squid and octopuses, have soft bodies and no backbone. Some, though, are able to grow shells. Snails and mussels are mollusks that grow shells.

OCTOPUS

SIZE: UP TO 16 FEET FROM ARM TO ARM AND WEIGHING UP TO 150 POUNDS

FAVORITE FOOD: CRABS AND MOLLUSKS

Octopuses live in all of Earth's oceans, from shallow water near the surface to the cold, deep ocean. They can weigh as little as an ounce or as much as 150 pounds. These mollusks have eight arms lined with suckers that they use to pull themselves along the ocean floor.

Unlike most of the world's creatures, octopuses have three hearts that pump blue blood through their bodies.

GIANT SQUID

SIZE: UP TO 60 FEET LONG AND WEIGHING UP TO 2,000 POUNDS

FAVORITE FOOD: FISH

HABITAT: OPEN OCEAN AROUND THE WORLD

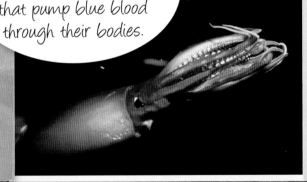

Squid have torpedo-shaped bodies that allow them to move quickly through the water. They suck water into their bodies and then force it out to propel themselves forward. This helps them avoid predators and catch prey.

INKED

Squid can camouflage themselves to hide from predators. They also release ink to quickly escape from predators.

ROCKY SHORE
ANIMAL PROFILES: SEALS AND SEA LIONS

Mammals are warm-blooded animals that have fur or hair, produce milk, and give birth to live young. Earth's oceans are home to many mammals, such as whales and dolphins. Seals and sea lions are mammals that live along the rocky shore.

SEA LIONS BASKING ON WARM ROCKS

SEAL AND SEA LION SNOOZE

Like other mammals, seals and sea lions have to swim to the ocean's surface for air. However, they can sleep underwater. They can even rise to the surface to breathe while they're asleep.

FLIPPER FEET

Seals and sea lions are *pinnipeds*, which means "flipper footed." This means that they have flippers instead of arms and legs. Their flippers are great for swimming, but they aren't very good for getting around on land.

SEA LION

SEAL

Although seals and sea lions look similar, there are a few differences between these two ocean mammals. Sea lions have a small flap over their ears, and seals only have ear holes.

SEA LION

FUR SEAL

SIZE: UP TO 10 FEET LONG AND WEIGHING UP TO 700 POUNDS

FAVORITE FOOD: FISH, SQUID, BIRDS, KRILL

Seals spend more time in the water than sea lions and may come ashore only once a year.

SEA LION

SIZE: UP TO 9 FEET LONG AND WEIGHING UP TO 2,400 POUNDS

FAVORITE FOOD: FISH, SQUID, OCTOPUS

Sea lions are more social than seals. They like to gather in large groups, called rookeries, along the rocky shore.

KELP FOREST

A kelp forest is an underwater forest made up of stalks of kelp, a large brown algae. They grow in shallow waters near the shore and grow like forests do on land. They provide food and shelter for many animals, such as sea otters, whales, and seagulls.

GROWING UP

Kelp forests grow in shallow water where there is plenty of sunlight. Giant kelp is the biggest seaweed and grows the quickest. It can grow 20 inches a day and over 100 feet long within a year.

FANTASTIC FOREST

Some animals use kelp to hide from their predators. Other animals find food in this forest, eating other fish or even the kelp.

In addition to providing shelter and food for thousands of plants and animals, many of us use kelp every day. From toothpaste to shampoo and even ice cream, kelp is an important ingredient in products. Kelp is made up of algin, a thickening ingredient necessary in a lot of the products we use.

ANIMAL PROFILES: SEA OTTERS

SEA OTTER

SIZE: 4 FEET AND WEIGHING UP TO 65 POUNDS

FAVORITE FOOD: CLAMS, MUSSELS, SEA URCHINS, CRABS, SQUID

HABITAT: COLD COASTAL WATERS OF THE NORTH PACIFIC OCEAN

Sea otters are playful mammals that love to swim in kelp forests. They can be seen diving among the kelp and playing with the things around them.

We are playful mammals! We like to flop around, wrestle, and chase our tails.

SEA OTTERS

DON'T DRIFT AWAY

When they aren't swimming in the kelp forest, sea otters like to float on top of it. They sleep on their backs side by side, wrapped in kelp to keep them from drifting away from each other. Some sea otters hold hands so they don't float apart from each other.

TOOL TIME

Sea otters are smart creatures that use tools like humans do. They hide rocks in an underarm pouch so they'll be handy when it's time to open a shell to get to the food inside. The sea otters will find a mussel or clam, swim back to the surface, and then use the rock to smash the shell open.

KEEPING WARM

Like manatees, sea otters don't have **blubber** to keep them warm. But sea otters are able to live in the cold ocean because their body has up to a million hairs per square inch, which keeps them warm.

THE OPEN OCEAN

The water that covers 70 percent of Earth's surface is divided into five oceans: the Pacific, Atlantic, Indian, Arctic, and Southern Oceans. Each ocean is home to many habitats and fascinating animals.

PACIFIC OCEAN

The Pacific Ocean is the largest and deepest ocean on Earth — it covers over 63,780,000 square miles. You could shove together all the continents in the world, and they still wouldn't be as big as the Pacific Ocean.

ATLANTIC OCEAN

The Atlantic Ocean is the youngest ocean at only 1.8 million years old. It separates North and South America from Europe and Africa.

ARCTIC OCEAN

The Arctic Ocean is the northernmost ocean and the smallest of Earth's oceans. The Arctic Ocean is so cold that it almost always has a thick layer of ice covering it.

INDIAN OCEAN

The Indian Ocean is the third largest ocean and the world's warmest. It is located between Africa, Australia, and Asia. The warm waters of the Indian Ocean are the world's largest breeding grounds for humpback whales.

SOUTHERN OCEAN

The Southern Ocean is the southernmost ocean and the second smallest ocean in the world. Also called the Antarctic Ocean, the Southern Ocean is the only ocean that wraps around the world.

THE MOTION OF THE OCEAN: CURRENTS

The ocean waters are constantly moving. On shore, the tides move water along with crashing waves. Water is also constantly on the move in the open ocean.

SEA TURTLES AND THE CURRENTS

If it weren't for Earth's warm currents, some sea turtles would not be able to survive. The water temperature of the currents is mild, and many sea turtles use the currents like a highway. Many sea turtle species lay their eggs on beaches far away from their favorite feeding grounds. Sea turtles will drift with the currents so they do not have to exert as much energy when migrating.

THE MOTION OF THE OCEAN

A current is a flow of water in a specific direction and pattern within the ocean. Warm and cold currents can be found all over Earth, and are caused by wind, gravity, and differences in salt content and temperature.

THE WORLD'S OCEAN CURRENTS

PLANT PROFILES

ALGAE

Algae can be found in all of the world's oceans. Algae are simple plants that grow in water and can be microscopic or over 100 feet in length. Algae can be found in three colors: brown, green, and red. Brown algae are the biggest and live in cold waters. Green algae need a lot of light, so they live in shallow water. Red algae live in tide pools, on coral reefs, and can live deeper in the ocean than other algae.

SEA GRASSES

Each ocean habitat supports different plants. Sea grasses grow in the shallow water along the coastline. Sea grasses are flowering plants that need a lot of light to grow and stay healthy.

PLANKTON

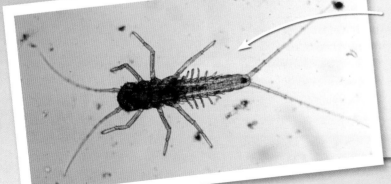

Plankton are plants, animals, and bacteria that are so small they can't be seen by the naked eye. They don't swim like other sea creatures; they move in the ocean with the tides and currents. Plankton may be small, but they are a major food source for many ocean creatures.

OPEN OCEAN: ANIMAL PROFILES

The open ocean is home to creatures large and small. Jellyfish, man-of-wars, and nudibranchs come in all different shapes and colors. Some can be as small as a human thumbnail, while others are as long as a school bus.

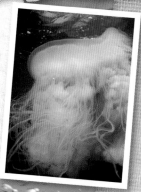

LONG LION'S MANE

The lion's mane jellyfish is the longest animal in the world. One lion's mane that washed ashore in Massachusetts had tentacles that were 120 feet long—longer than a blue whale.

KRILL

SIZE: UP TO 2 INCHES LONG

FAVORITE FOOD: PHYTOPLANKTON

Krill are small, shrimplike creatures that feed hundreds of animals in the open ocean, from small fish to the gigantic blue whale. Krill play an important role in the food chain.

Jellyfish are one of the oldest creatures on Earth; they have been around since before the dinosaurs. Their bodies are 97 percent water and they do not have brains, hearts, or bones. They have a bell-shaped body with long, stinging tentacles attached.

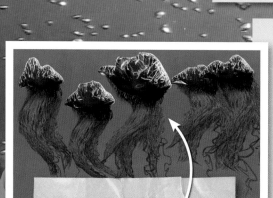

Man-of-wars look like jellyfish, but they are made up of a colony of many creatures. They float near the ocean surface in tropical oceans around the world. Like jellyfish, man-of-wars have long, stinging tentacles that are used to stun their prey.

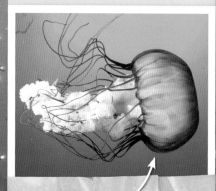

MAN-OF-WAR

SIZE: UP TO 165 FEET LONG

FAVORITE FOOD: FISH

JELLYFISH

SIZE: UP TO 98 FEET LONG AND WEIGHING UP TO 550 POUNDS

FAVORITE FOOD: FISH, SHRIMP, CRABS, TINY PLANTS

NUDIBRANCH

SIZE: UP TO 12 INCHES LONG

FAVORITE FOOD: ALGAE, SPONGES, ANEMONES, CORALS, BARNACLES

Nudibranchs are colorful, shell-less mollusks that are part of the sea slug family. They are found throughout the world's oceans, but can often be found in warm, shallow water. Nudibranchs' coloring and camouflage depends on the types of food they eat. They eat algae, sponges, anemones, corals, and barnacles.

Lampreys are eel-like fish that have been living on Earth since before the dinosaurs. They are parasitic fish, meaning they attach themselves to other fish for blood and body fluids. They have round, suckerlike mouths full of sharp teeth that they use to latch onto their victim.

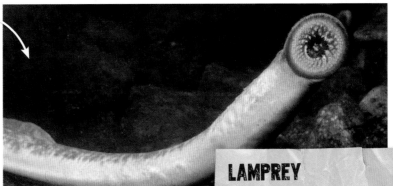

LAMPREY

SIZE: UP TO 40 INCHES LONG

FAVORITE FOOD: FISH

SEA CUCUMBER

SIZE: UP TO 6 FEET LONG

FAVORITE FOOD: ALGAE

Sea cucumbers have a long body like a cucumber, and are related to sea stars and sea urchins. When feeding, they use the 30 tube feet that surround their mouth to gather food. If they are threatened, sea cucumbers can use sticky threads to catch their predators.

OPEN OCEAN:
ANIMAL PROFILES: SEA TURTLES

Sea turtles are reptiles. They have a hard shell and flippers that propel them through the water. Sea turtles migrate long distances to lay eggs on the beach. Unlike land turtles, sea turtles are unable to hide their head, tail, and flippers in their shell.

Leatherback sea turtles are unlike other sea turtles because they do not have a hard shell. Instead, their shells are leathery and flexible, which is why they are called "leatherback." Leatherback sea turtles are the largest turtles in the world.

EGGS HERE OR THERE

Some sea turtles nest and lay eggs in one place, while others swim thousands of miles to lay eggs.

LEATHERBACK SEA TURTLE

SIZE: UP TO 7 FEET LONG AND WEIGHING UP TO 2,000 POUNDS

FAVORITE FOOD: JELLYFISH

HABITAT: OPEN OCEAN AROUND THE WORLD

Each year, leatherback sea turtles migrate thousands of miles to and from the warm beaches where they lay eggs.

BABY LEATHERBACK TURTLES

LOGGERHEAD SEA TURTLE

SIZE: UP TO 3 FEET LONG AND WEIGHING UP TO 250 POUNDS

FAVORITE FOOD: JELLYFISH, CONCHS, CRABS, FISH

HABITAT: OPEN OCEAN AROUND THE WORLD

Loggerhead sea turtles travel up to 1,400 miles to lay eggs. They migrate to the same beach where they hatched. A female loggerhead sea turtle may lay eggs up to seven times a year. Each nest has 100–120 eggs.

The green sea turtle is one of the largest sea turtles in the world. Although it has a large body, its head is quite small. They have strong flippers that look like paddles that help them move through the water.

GREEN SEA TURTLE

SIZE: UP TO 5 FEET LONG AND WEIGHING UP TO 700 POUNDS

FAVORITE FOOD: SEA GRASSES, ALGAE

HABITAT: TROPICAL AND SUBTROPICAL OCEANS

OLIVE RIDLEY SEA TURTLE

SIZE: UP TO 2.5 FEET LONG AND WEIGHING UP TO 100 POUNDS

FAVORITE FOOD: JELLYFISH, SNAILS, CRABS, SHRIMP

HABITAT: WARM WATERS OF THE ATLANTIC, PACIFIC, AND INDIAN OCEANS

The olive ridley sea turtle is named for the green coloring of its shell and skin. Every few years olive ridley sea turtles travel thousands of miles to the beach where the mother turtle hatched. Thousands of olive ridley sea turtles come ashore to lay eggs.

OPEN OCEAN:
ANIMAL PROFILES: FISH

Fish are cold-blooded animals that can be found in both fresh and salt water. Because they do not come up to the surface to breathe, fish have gills that they use to flush oxygen into their bodies. Fish are usually covered in scales and have fins that help them move through the water. From warm, shallow water to the deepest, darkest depths, fish can be found in every part of the ocean.

FLYING FISH

SIZE: UP TO 18 INCHES LONG

FAVORITE FOOD: PLANKTON

NOWHERE TO HIDE

In the open ocean, there are no coral reefs to hide in or kelp forests to swim through. The animals that swim in the open ocean use many techniques to protect themselves from predators. Some creatures camouflage themselves, while others have stinging tentacles that ward off predators. Some can even swim so fast that they break the ocean's surface and can "fly" through the air, out of a predator's reach!

Once they speed up through the water and launch into the air, flying fish can soar for 600 feet before diving back into the ocean.

Flying fish have torpedo-shaped bodies that help them move fast through the water. Fins located on the sides of their bodies act as wings once the flying fish breaks the ocean's surface.

TUNA

SIZE: UP TO 6.5 FEET LONG AND WEIGHING UP TO 550 POUNDS

FAVORITE FOOD: SMALLER FISH, CRUSTACEANS, SQUID, EELS

Tuna can be large or small, and some can weigh more than a horse. They have torpedo-shaped bodies and special fins and scales that help them move through the water. Tuna can swim as fast as 43 miles per hour. Tuna also gather in schools in order to protect themselves from predators. When fish are in a large school, it's harder for a predator to pick out just one fish to attack, so there is safety in a school.

Blue marlins are giant fish found in the open ocean. They have blue and silver coloring and a long, spear-shaped upper jaw. Blue marlins are fast swimmers that use their sharp jaw to slice into schools of fish. After the attack, the blue marlin eats the wounded fish.

BLUE MARLIN

SIZE: UP TO 14 FEET LONG AND WEIGHING UP TO 2,000 POUNDS

FAVORITE FOOD: MACKEREL AND TUNA

MOLA

SIZE: UP TO 14 FEET LONG AND WEIGHING UP TO 5,000 POUNDS

FAVORITE FOOD: JELLYFISH, SMALL FISH, ALGAE

Molas are one of the strangest fish in the sea. They have enormous, flat bodies—up to 14 feet long! They are also the world's heaviest bony fish, weighing 5,000 pounds. Molas' tall, silver dorsal fins have been mistaken for shark fins!

OPEN OCEAN:
ANIMAL PROFILES: SHARKS

Some of the world's most ferocious and aggressive creatures live in the open ocean: sharks. More than 400 species of sharks live in the ocean. They live in the deep ocean and in shallow coastal waters. Each shark has special features that make it unique.

TERRIFYING TEETH

Sharks are often feared because of their many sharp teeth. If a shark loses a tooth, it will replace it. In fact, they have rows of teeth waiting in line. Great white sharks have 3,000 teeth in their mouth at all times.

FEARSOME FISH

Sharks are a type of fish. Like other fish, sharks swim by moving their bodies from side to side. Sharks need to swim in order to live; they get the oxygen they need from the water around them.

GREAT WHITE SHARK

SIZE: UP TO 20 FEET LONG AND WEIGHING UP TO 5,000 POUNDS

FAVORITE FOOD: SEA LIONS, SEALS, SMALL TOOTHED WHALES

The great white shark is one of the most feared and aggressive sharks on the planet. This shark is responsible for up to half of the shark attacks on humans each year. Great white sharks have amazing senses—they can detect blood from three miles away!

One of the most unique sharks is the hammerhead. It has a wide, long head with one eye and nostril on each end. The shape of its head helps it pin down stingrays on the ocean floor before eating them.

HAMMERHEAD SHARK

SIZE: UP TO 20 FEET LONG AND WEIGHING UP TO 1,000 POUNDS

FAVORITE FOOD: STINGRAYS

Tiger sharks are vicious sharks that can be 25 feet long. They have sharp teeth that help them rip through the shells of sea turtles. Tiger sharks have been known to attack humans.

TIGER SHARK

SIZE: UP TO 14 FEET LONG AND WEIGHING UP TO 1,400 POUNDS

FAVORITE FOOD: STINGRAYS, SEALS, SQUID

OPEN OCEAN:
ANIMAL PROFILES:
DOLPHINS AND PORPOISES

Ocean mammals live in all parts of the ocean, from the icy waters of the Arctic to the rocky shore. The open ocean is home to many mammals, such as dolphins, porpoises, and whales.

BREATH OF FRESH AIR

Whales, dolphins, and porpoises may look like fish, but they're mammals, just like seals and sea lions. Because they are mammals, they must come up to the surface to breathe. While fish use gills to breathe, dolphins and porpoises have nostrils called blowholes located on top of their heads.

Dolphins are small toothed whales. They communicate with other dolphins using whistles, clicks, chirps, and by slapping their tail. When dolphins make these noises, they are saying they are happy, sad, scared, or want to play.

BOTTLENOSE DOLPHIN

SIZE: UP TO 14 FEET LONG AND WEIGHING UP TO 1,100 POUNDS

FAVORITE FOOD: SHRIMP, SQUID

HABITAT: OPEN OCEAN AND WARM COASTAL WATERS AROUND THE WORLD

WHAT'S YOUR NAME?
Dolphins also use noises to identify each other. This is like calling each other by a name.

HARBOR PORPOISE

SIZE: UP TO 6.5 FEET LONG AND WEIGHING UP TO 200 POUNDS

FAVORITE FOOD: FISH

HABITAT: COOL COASTAL WATERS

A dolphin's mouth is full of sharp teeth. Porpoises do not have as many teeth. Their teeth are flatter, but they are still sharp!

Dolphins and porpoises are an important part of the food chain. Unfortunately, humans are responsible for many of the injuries and deaths of dolphins and porpoises each year. It is estimated that 300,000 whales and dolphins die each year because of fishing nets. Other deaths occur due to pollution or habitat loss.

FISH OR MAMMAL?

You can tell the difference between a fish and a mammal by how they swim. Mammals, such as whales and dolphins, pump their tails up and down to swim. Fish wave their tails from side to side.

OPEN OCEAN:
ANIMAL PROFILES: WHALES

Whales are the largest creatures in the oceans. Whales are mammals, just like dolphins, porpoises, seals, and sea lions. They have to swim up to the ocean's surface to breathe. Like dolphins, whales use different noises to communicate with each other, find their way in the ocean, and hunt for food.

WAILING WHALES

Whales communicate with each other by making clicking, grunting, humming, and moaning noises. These noises also help them travel and find food. Sometimes, these songs can be heard by other whales 50 miles away.

FOOD STRAINER

Most whale species swallow their food whole without chewing it. They have plates on their gums that are fringed and act like a strainer. This allows water to flow out of the whale's mouth so they can swallow their favorite food, krill.

BLUE WHALE

SIZE: UP TO 105 FEET LONG AND WEIGHING UP TO 400,000 POUNDS

FAVORITE FOOD: KRILL

HABITAT: OPEN OCEAN

Blue whales are the biggest animals that have ever been on Earth— bigger than any dinosaur. When they are born, they are 25 feet long. As an adult, a blue whale's heart is the size of a small car and its tongue weighs as much as an elephant. Although they are the largest animal, they eat one of the smallest—krill.

HUMPBACK WHALE

SIZE: UP TO 62 FEET LONG AND WEIGHING UP TO 80,000 POUNDS

FAVORITE FOOD: KRILL, PLANKTON, SMALL FISH

HABITAT: OPEN OCEAN

The sperm whale has a large head with a rounded forehead. They have the largest brain of any creature to ever live on Earth.

Humpback whales are large whales that grow to be 62 feet long. They migrate each year from the poles to the equator. They use their strong tail fin to launch themselves out of the water belly-up.

SPERM WHALE

SIZE: UP TO 59 FEET LONG AND WEIGHING UP TO 90,000 POUNDS

FAVORITE FOOD: SQUID

HABITAT: OPEN OCEAN

ICY WATERS

The Arctic and Antarctic Oceans surround the most northern and southern points on Earth. These chilly oceans are home to animals that have adapted to icy waters.

HOME ON THE ICE

The Arctic Ocean is home to a rich variety of animals. Polar bears and their cubs live on the ice and dive into the water to catch prey. Narwhals' tusks can be seen as they swim near the surface of the water. Walruses gather in groups on the ice.

PENGUIN PARTY

The Antarctic Ocean's ice is a popular gathering place for penguins. They huddle in large colonies on the frozen landscape and swim in the ocean for most of the day.

TIP OF THE ICEBERG

The Arctic and Antarctic Oceans are full of ice called icebergs. Icebergs are large chunks of glaciers that have broken off and float in the ocean. Sometimes, only the tip of an iceberg can be seen on the ocean's surface. Icebergs can be dangerous to ships, since most of the ice is not visible from the water's surface.

CHANGING CLIMATE, CHANGING CONDITIONS

Climate is the conditions of an area on Earth over a long period of time. The climate on Earth is changing and temperatures are getting warmer because of human activity. The burning of fossil fuels and cutting down of forests has affected weather and temperatures all over the world.

Because temperatures on Earth are getting warmer, the ice and snow in the Arctic and Antarctic is melting. This not only causes the ocean levels to rise, but lessens the amount of ice available for polar bears and other animals to live on.

ICY WATERS: ANIMAL PROFILES

Many animals call the Arctic home. From walruses to seals to polar bears, these animals have special features so they can live in freezing temperatures.

WALRUS

SIZE: UP TO 11.5 FEET LONG AND WEIGHING UP TO 3,000 POUNDS

FAVORITE FOOD: SHELLFISH

HABITAT: COLD ARCTIC WATERS

The walrus is a large mammal that lives near the Arctic Circle. They are known for their large tusks that grow from their whiskery mouths. Their tusks can grow to be three feet long.

WALRUS GATHERING

Walruses love to live in large groups. They can be seen lounging on the ice with over 100 walruses. There they noisily bask in the sun, grunting and snorting with their companions.

WARM AND COZY

Walruses have large, lumbering bodies that can weigh over 3,000 pounds. Like other ocean mammals, walruses have blubber, a layer of fat on their bodies that keeps them warm in the cold temperatures of the Arctic.

NARWHAL

SIZE: UP TO 20 FEET LONG AND WEIGHING UP TO 3,500 POUNDS

FAVORITE FOOD: FISH, SHRIMP, SQUID

HABITAT: COLD ARCTIC WATERS

Narwhals are called "unicorns of the sea" because of the tusk that grows from male narwhals' upper lips. The tusks are used in mating rituals to impress the female and to battle other males.

FAMILY TREE

Narwhals are related to dolphins, porpoises, and orcas. They travel in groups and feed on fish, shrimp, and squid.

Beluga whales are white whales related to narwhals. They have rounded foreheads and a portly body. Beluga whales are the only whales that can turn their head to the side.

BELUGA WHALE

SIZE: UP TO 20 FEET LONG AND WEIGHING UP TO 3,000 POUNDS

FAVORITE FOOD: FISH, CRUSTACEANS, WORMS

HABITAT: COLD ARCTIC WATERS

PLAYTIME

Beluga whales are social animals that hunt and migrate in groups. They are also playful mammals that enjoy chasing and rubbing against other belugas.

ICY WATERS:
ANIMAL PROFILES:
POLAR BEARS AND PENGUINS

Some animals may not spend their entire lives in the ocean — like fish, octopuses, and sharks — but the ocean habitat plays an important role in their lives.

POLAR BEAR

SIZE: UP TO 8 FEET LONG AND WEIGHING UP TO 1,600 POUNDS

FAVORITE FOOD: SEALS, WHALES

HABITAT: LAND AROUND THE ARCTIC CIRCLE

Polar bears can be found in the Arctic Circle. Although they live on land, polar bears are excellent swimmers.

NOT A HAIR OUT OF PLACE

Polar bears may look like they are covered in white hair, but their hair is actually clear, hollow tubes. They have bumps and hair on their feet that help them walk on ice so they don't slip.

MOTHER AND BABIES

Unlike other bears, polar bears do not hibernate. Hibernation is a period of rest when the winter weather is harsh. Only pregnant female polar bears build dens in the winter. Here the mother gives birth and raises her cubs until spring.

JOIN THE CROWD

Penguins are social birds. During breeding season, they form large groups called rookeries.

DIVE IN

Penguins are flightless birds that spend most of their time swimming in the ocean. They live in the southern portion of the world. They dive into the water to catch their favorite foods: krill, fish, and squid.

ON THE MOVE!

Although they can't fly, penguins move in many different ways. Penguins stand on two feet like humans do. On ice, they waddle on their feet. When they are tired of waddling, penguins slide on their bellies.

EMPEROR PENGUIN

SIZE: UP TO 45 INCHES TALL AND WEIGHING UP TO 88 POUNDS

FAVORITE FOOD: FISH, SQUID, KRILL

HABITAT: ANTARCTICA

Emperor penguins are the largest type of penguin. They live on the chilly ice of Antarctica. To keep warm, groups of penguins huddle together to escape the harsh Antarctic winds.

ADÉLIE PENGUIN

SIZE: UP TO 28 INCHES TALL AND WEIGHING UP TO 12 POUNDS

FAVORITE FOOD: KRILL, SHRIMP, SQUID

HABITAT: ANTARCTICA

Like other penguins, Adélie penguins are flightless birds that are excellent swimmers. They can swim up to 185 miles round-trip searching for food. During breeding season, Adélie penguins gather in a colony, a large group of up to 1,000 penguins. There they build nests for their eggs out of small stones.

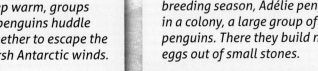

THE DEEP SEA

Coasts and reefs are fairly easy to explore, but scientists are still investigating the deepest, darkest parts of the oceans. Here, there is no light. The creatures that live in the deep sea must make their own light.

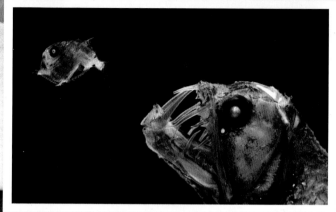

IN TOO DEEP

The deepest part of the Pacific Ocean is Challenger Deep in the Mariana **Trench**. The Mariana Trench is 36,198 feet deep. It is the deepest location on Earth. It is very cold and dark in the trench, but it is home to thousands of sea creatures.

MARIANA TRENCH

If you were standing on the floor of the Mariana Trench, you would feel more than 8 tons of pressure per square inch. That would be like trying to hold up 50 airplanes!

UNDERSEA HOT SPRINGS

Hot, liquefied rock found beneath Earth's surface is called magma. Magma seeps out of the space created by the moving plates on Earth's crust. The magma and the ocean water create hot springs. Although they are located deep in the ocean, the rich minerals that come out of the vents allow life to thrive without sunlight.

ANIMAL PROFILES

The deep, dark sea is home to some of the strangest creatures on the planet. The fish that inhabit the dark depths have special body parts that they use to find mates or prey, or to scare predators away. These fish have adapted to life without sunlight.

The viperfish has a long, thin body like an eel. It has very sharp teeth that are so long, the viperfish cannot shut its mouth. The viperfish produces glowing spots on its body to attract prey.

VIPERFISH
SIZE: UP TO 2 FEET LONG
FAVORITE FOOD: CRUSTACEANS, SMALL FISH

ANGLERFISH
SIZE: UP TO 3 FEET LONG
FAVORITE FOOD: FISH

Anglerfish live in the deep Atlantic and Antarctic Oceans. The female anglerfish has a spine attached to the top of her head like a fishing pole. The end of the spine has a light that is used to attract prey. Their mouth is so big that they can swallow prey twice their size.

FANGTOOTH FISH
SIZE: UP TO 6 INCHES LONG
FAVORITE FOOD: FISH, CRUSTACEANS

Many creatures living in the darkest ocean waters make their own light. This is called **bioluminescence.**

The fangtooth fish lives so deep that the water temperature is nearly freezing. It has a short body with a giant mouth filled with long, sharp teeth. Fangtooth fish have poor eyesight and swim around until they bump into prey.

GLOSSARY

Bioluminescence: the shining of light from a living being

Blubber: a layer of fat that marine mammals use for warmth and energy

Camouflage: an animal's coloring and texture that enables it to blend in with its surroundings

Colony: a living structure created by a group of organisms

Crustaceans: animals covered in a hard outer shell that live on land, in freshwater, or in the sea.

Food chain: the order in which animals eat plants and other animals

Habitats: environments in which plants and animals live

Mammals: animals that produce milk to feed their young, and are usually covered in fur or hair

Migration: the movement of animals across long distances

Oceans: large bodies of salt water

Polyps: coral tiny, soft-bodied coral organisms

Predator: animal that hunts other animals for food

Prey: animals that are hunted by other animals for food

Reef: a ridge of rock, coral, or sand that is at or just under the ocean's surface

Sea level: the surface level of the ocean halfway between low and high tide; used to measure elevation and depth

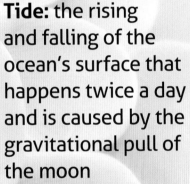

Tentacles: long, flexible, armlike body parts on the head or around the mouth of some animals, like an octopus, and used for grabbing and moving

Tide: the rising and falling of the ocean's surface that happens twice a day and is caused by the gravitational pull of the moon

Trench: a long, narrow cut in Earth's surface

Tube feet: projections located on the bottom of sea stars' arms that help them move and stick to surfaces

3-D Model Instructions

Complete one model at a time. Press out the pieces and arrange them as shown. Using the numbers on the pictures here, match the slots and assemble your 3-D ocean animals.

Sailfish

Sailfish are the fastest fish in the ocean, reaching a top speed of 68 miles per hour.

1. Line up the slots.

2. Push fin piece through all three slots.

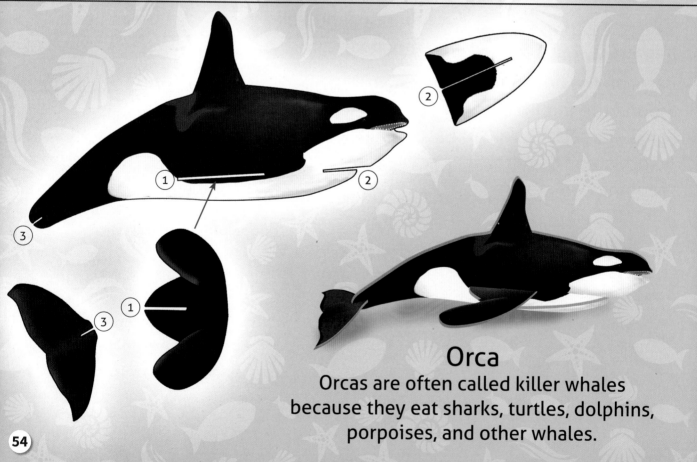

Orca

Orcas are often called killer whales because they eat sharks, turtles, dolphins, porpoises, and other whales.

Great White Shark
The great white shark is one of the biggest sharks and can grow to be up to 23 feet long.

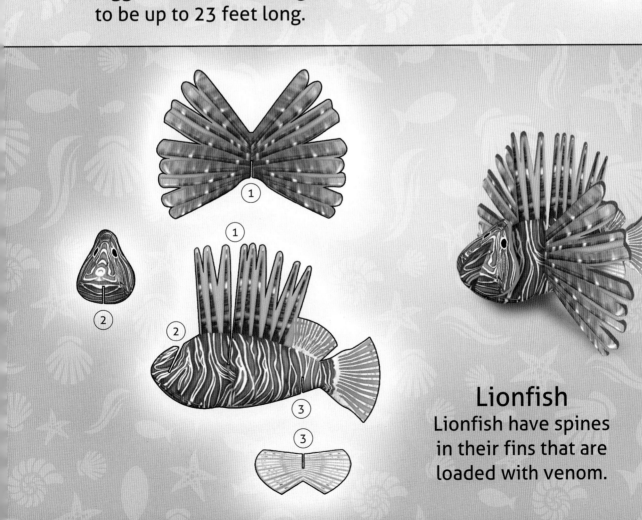

Lionfish
Lionfish have spines in their fins that are loaded with venom.

Diorama Instructions

Bring your own ocean world to life by building a beautiful diorama. It's easy!

1. The inside of the box lid and base will be the walls of your diorama. The unfolding board will be the floor. Decorate these with reusable stickers as desired.

2. Press out the floor figures, and fold as shown. Decorate with some stickers if desired. Fold, then slide the rectangular tabs through the floor slots, folding them underneath so the figures stand upright. The tabs and slots are all the same size, so you can change the position of the figures.

3. Stand the box lid and base upright and at an angle as shown. Lay the angled back edges of the floor piece on top of the box sides. You're done!

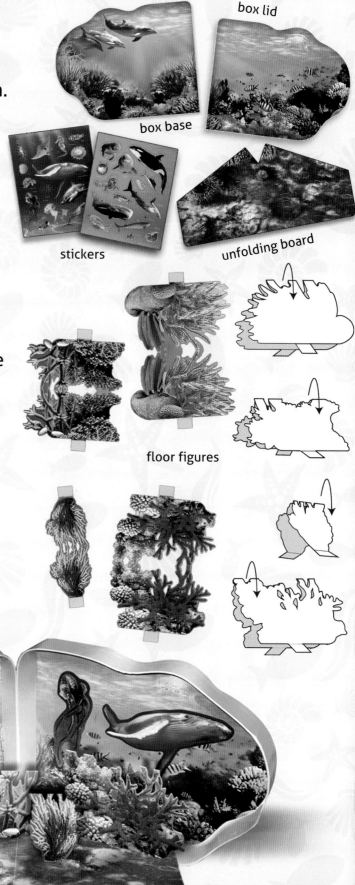

box lid

box base

stickers

unfolding board

floor figures